YOUR BEAUTIFUL HOME

ADORNING HOMECRAFTS FOR EACH ROOM

C.R.Gibson®

FINE GIFTS SINCE 1870

INTRODUCTION

GOLDFINCHES ARE KNOWN to decorate their nests with a spray of forget-me-nots and a fern frond or two in the interests of promoting a happy home life. If they feel moved to such efforts, there is every reason why humans should enjoy the pleasures of adding a touch of paint or a waft of fabric to their homes. Decorating is one of life's most innocent and cheering pastimes; there is little to compare with the heady excitement of turning a junk-shop discovery into an heirloom, or a bundle of sale remnants into a sumptuous cushion. This is how good, warm feelings begin, and how a house magically transmutes into a home. This book is intended to be a confidence booster, to demonstrate that you do not have to be an interior designer to make your home look stunning.

ORGANIZATION AND INSPIRATION

Once you have settled on a color scheme to follow, but before you begin to make anything, look afresh at your existing possessions. You could recycle the things you can't bear to part with – throw out the chipped, broken, and tattered with a great sigh of relief, and make the most of those things that give enduring pleasure. Men's old pinstriped cotton shirts make extremely stylish patchwork quilts, and brushed cotton checks in related colors can be pieced in simple squares and knotted to a cotton interlining to make deliciously cozy winter curtains.

If you have amassed lots of clutter and would like either to hide it or alternatively to show it off, try building or painting shelves or frames in which to flatter it, or boxes in which to conceal it. Displaying collections of favorite objects is best served by editing them down first to those that look good together. There are plenty of examples shown in the book, and, once you start, you will come up with ideas of your own.

Typically a home does not require a major face-lift to enhance its qualities. In fact, the small touches can produce the most dramatic effects. And remember that a personal expression of creativity or a framed keepsake always means more than an item purchased in a store.

2

One of the great pleasures of making things for your home is starting from scratch; this is where searching through magazines for great color partnerships or motifs to steal comes into its own. The vibrant Persian table rug in a Holbein painting may provide inspiration for shades and tones that you might use on your own tablecloth. French and American folk art is rich with ideas for decorative details to plagiarize for naive freehand finishes. You will soon discover that your immediate surroundings are a constant source of inspiration.

ENJOYING YOURSELF

Making things for your home is quite simply thrilling. Mastering any of the manageable skills required to paint a box or stitch a cushion requires total concentration, and the complete absorption of creating something from scratch will make time fly. Whatever mysterious human need is satisfied by making things, the effect is cumulative – the more you do, the more you *can* do.

GETTING STARTED

Most of the projects in this book can be made quickly, and if you can evict the children for the best part of a single day, there is a good chance you will have finished by the time they return to mess with the glue and knock over your paint.

One of the most compelling reasons to make things yourself is the fact that your work will be uniquely yours. You can make whatever you like exactly as you want it. So, if the urge seizes you, start today. You probably already have half the materials on hand, and just need a nudge to assemble something terrific. Making something is such a pleasure in itself, it is a glorious bonus if you end up with something usable and attractive.

*T*he quickest way to beautify
your home is to decorate it
with love.

*H*allways are the paths that lead to the rooms of your home. Decorative touches along the walls are a vital part of connecting your creative efforts throughout the rest of your house.

ENTRANCES & EXITS

GILDED MIRROR FRAME

GILDED MIRROR FRAME

MATERIALS

- Mirror frame and mirror
- Mounting board
- Bronze powder
- PVA glue
- Water
- Gold powder
- Gold wrapping paper
- Gold transfer paper

THIS FRAME is a glittering example of making little into plenty – the materials are cheap and easy to come by, and the effect is of positively Byzantine richness, combined with a hint of Mayan mystery. This mirror also has the extra advantage of framing faces in something glamorous – offering your guests a warm welcome or gracious exit. It is simple to make and requires just a modicum of skill in the shaping and cutting. The decoration needs only a steady hand and a dash of panache.

Gilt Options

Rich, tawny shades of bronze and a splash of speckled with different [...] of gold make this humb[...] frame luxurious. Blue, purple, ruby, and silver would have a grand and opulent effect.

A mirror is a necessary tool for fixing your hair, adjusting your tie, checking your make-up . . .

[M]AKING THE FRAME

[D]esigning the frame
[D]raw the shape of your
[mirro]r frame on mounting
[boar]d. Center a semicircle on
[the t]op edge of the frame.
[Care]fully cut out the penciled
[shap]e using a craft or utility
[knife.] Be sure to protect your
[work] surface with a cutting
[mat] or a piece of cardboard.

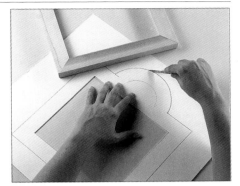

2 Painting the frame
Using PVA glue, attach the mounting
board shape to the frame. Mix bronze powder
with a little PVA glue and water until it is the
consistency of cream. Paint this on to the
semicircular area of the mounting board. With a
mix of gold powder, PVA glue, and water, paint
the rest of the board. Leave to dry.

[D]ECORATING THE FRAME

2 Enriching the collage
Embellish the decoration further
by gluing small squares of wrapping
paper and gold transfer
paper around the edge
of the frame. For
a matte effect,
leave the backing
paper in place on
some of the squares
of gold transfer paper.
Leave to dry.

[G]luing on gold strips
[T]ear or cut gold wrapping paper
[into] small strips about 1 in (2.5 cm)
[long] and ¼ in (6 mm) wide. Paint each
[one] individually with PVA glue and
[glue] them around the inner edge of the
[fram]e. Repeat to decorate the outer
[edge]s of the frame.

[S]coring the frame
[U]sing the back of a craft knife
[blad]e, make decorative scratches,
[squ]iggles, and scored
[line]s on the frame.
[Inse]rt the mirror in
[the] frame and hang
[it in] a place of honor
[on] the wall.

> ... but in the right frame
> it can also be the perfect
> reflection of who you are.

*A*ptly named, most frequently used, always
in need of a good polish. The living room
is where comfort and practicality are as
important as your design touches.

THE LIVING ROOM

CRACKLED LAMP BASE

KALEIDOSCOPE CUSHION

CRACKLED LAMP BASE

MATERIALS

- Wooden lamp base
- Mulberry latex paint
- Acrylic water-based varnish
- Gold acrylic paint
- Two-part crackle varnish
- Gold oil paint
- Oil-based varnish

RICH, DARK COLORS, with a discreet haze of antiqued gold, contribute a classic dignity to a table lamp. The shape has a vague look of the Empire about it, and you could do worse than partner it with a thick cream shade of handmade paper sporting a stenciled laurel wreath. The nimble-fingered could attach the paper shade to the frame with mulberry cord and tassels.

A simple finish, such as the one shown here, is manageable on such a curvaceous shape, whereas stencils, other than the tiniest of motifs, would be tricky. It is perfectly possible, if you have a steady hand, to achieve something more ambitious by painting on freehand bands, stripes, or dots.

Bands of Gold

Subtle gilding enlivens the somber good looks of the lamp base. The effect is formal – a matching pa would radiate gravitas a well as twice the wattag You could echo the colo elsewhere to make a harmonious theme – in other lamps, in frames, boxes – to be picked up with upholstery fabrics and cushions.

DECORATING THE BASE

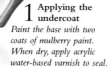

1 Applying the undercoat
Paint the base with two coats of mulberry paint. When dry, apply acrylic water-based varnish to seal.

2 Painting gold decoration
Using an artist's brush, paint rings of gold acryl paint around the lamp base, following the shap the molding. Allow to d

3 Applying crackle varnish
Apply the first solution of crackle varnish. Let dry, following the manufacturer's instructions. Using a soft-haired synthetic brush, apply the second solution of crackle varnish; let dry.

4 Rubbing in paint
Using a pad of paper towels, gently rub gold oil paint into the cracks that have appeared in the painted surface.

5 Cleaning and varnishing
Using a fresh pad of paper, rub awa the paint to reveal the gold cracks beneat Allow the paint to dry for a few days. T apply oil-based varnish to seal the surfac

*L*ate night reading.
Late night snacking.
Late night solitude. All are
served better when the light
is clear, clean, and bright.
Thank-you, Mr. Edison.

KALEIDOSCOPE CUSHION

A living room pillow is much like a sleek race horse: Beautiful to look at, easy to handle, but not entirely practical for more than one person at a time.

MATERIALS
- Paper and cardboard
- 4 20in (50cm) squares of silk or rayon
- Fusible webbing
- 25 x 20in (62.5 x 50cm) gold silk
- Plaid taffeta
- Multicolored rayon thread
- Purple and red silk
- 2 20in (50cm) squares of silk for backing
- 25 x 20in (62.5 x 50cm) cushion pad
- Silk strips for tassels
- Narrow ribbon
- Silk organza

I F YOU HAVE EVER been lured inexorably to the seemingly useless but opulent fabric remnants in a sale, you will find that this cushion cover puts those scraps to perfect use. It is a glamorous example of the whole being far greater than the parts, and can be as elegant and baroque as your scrap bag suggests. If your taste inclines more to natural and countrified, you could adapt the technique for calico and gingham, spotted bandannas and tassels of twine – or go all out for feminine charm and create something rich and luxe from satins, silk, ribbons, and lace. The motifs can be either regular or random – this grid design gives the beginner a comforting sense of structure, but appliqué can be as free as you like.

*Harlequin Patch
The appliqués on thes
cushions (right) draw
on a childishly simple
repertoire of motifs,
but the result is rich
and sophisticated.*

PREPARING THE FABRIC

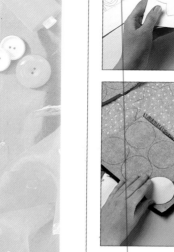

1 Cutting templates
Sketch out the design for your cushion on a piece of paper. This simple grid features a combination of stars, spirals, and circles in each square. On a piece of cardboard, draw a star 5in (12.5cm) wide and a circle 3in (7.5cm) in diameter, and cut them out to make templates for the appliquéd shapes.

2 Applying backin
*Place a 20in (50cm
or rayon square right sid
down. Lay fusible web
on top, sticky side do
Run a warm iron
this for a few sec
until the adhes
darkens. Repe
process on th
more squa*

3 Marking motifs
Using a pencil, draw around the star template six times on each of two fabric squares – here a spotted rayon and a rayon print. Then draw around the circle template six times on each of the two remaining squares – here, a plain red silk and a very dark green silk.

4 Cutting out appliqué motifs
Cut out the motifs; the fusible webb should remain attached. You should now 12 star and 12 circle motifs.

ASSEMBLING THE DESIGN

1 Assembling the grid
Lay the 25 x 20in (62.5 x 50cm) panel of gold silk down, right side up. Referring to the design sketch, lay three strips of plaid taffeta lengthwise and four strips widthwise across the silk to form a grid with 20 squares. Pin the taffeta strips in place.

2 Stitching strips
Thread a sewing machine with multicolored rayon thread, or colored cotton thread if you prefer. Stitch each strip to the gold silk with two lines of straight stitching (see inset). Remove the pins.

3 Positioning motifs
Arrange the star and circle motifs in the two outer vertical rows and the central vertic row of squares, alternating the different color of fabric. Peel the fusible webbing paper backing off each motif, then place the motifs position. Place the circles on top of the stars.

4 Fusing motifs
Iron the motifs in place as you go with a warm iron. The heat melts the webbing and fuses the motifs to the silk. Repeat until all the motifs are attached to the cushion front.

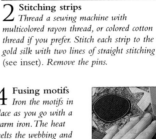

5 Stitching motifs
Using multicolored rayon thread or colore cotton thread, machin stitch two rows of straight stitching around each star. Then stitch one row of straight stitching around each circle. You could use a darning foot here if you prefer

6 Stitching silk spirals
Stitch a torn strip of purple silk in a spiral in one of the remaining squares. Then stitch a spiral of torn red silk in the next square. Repeat to fill all the remaining squares of the grid with alternating purple and red silk spirals.

7 Decorating the circles
Stitch a torn strip of red silk in a spiral on top of one of the appliquéd circles. The stitch a spiral of torn purple silk on the ne appliquéd circle. Rep this process on all the remaining circles, alternating red and purple silk strips as before.

MAKING THE BACKING

Positioning backing pieces
Place two 20in (50cm) squares of contrasting-ed silk on top of the gold silk, right sides facing appliqués. The two squares should overlap in the dle. Fold back each overlapping end twice, so the ends overlap by t 5in (12.5cm).

Stitching backing
Pin the backing pieces e gold silk along all sides. Stitch around edges with cotton ad. Remove the pins. the cushion cover right out through the central lapping flap. Insert a x 20in (62.5 x m) cushion pad.

MAKING A TASSEL

For a finishing flourish, add a tassel to each corner of the cushion. They are easy to make with scraps of silk and can be attached using a few hand stitches.

1 Lay a bunch of 10 colored silk strips, 10in (25cm) long, on a flat surface. Tie them in the middle with a narrow ribbon or silk strip.

2 Fold the strips in half so that the tied ribbon is at the center. Using a 10in (25cm) strip of silk organza, tie a bow around the folded silk strips, about ½in (12mm) below the fold.

3 Trim the ends of the silk tassel to the desired length. Repeat to make three more tassels.

DESIGN OPTIONS

Diamond Lattice
Stitched stripes are the base for this small square cushion (below). A grid of strips was stitched diagonally over them and the regular intersections punctuated by giant cross stitches. Against this background, multicolored rosettes were appliquéd, producing an effect that is both formal and spontaneous.

aves and Flowers
is cushion (above) appears to have all carefree spontaneity of a child's drawing, it has been carefully considered and lt up in many layers on a bright chwork of colors. Hand stitching a strong element of this design.

Patches and Petals
The foundation for this medium-sized square cushion (left) is a silk patchwork consisting of a central block surrounded by 12 smaller squares. A regular lattice of fabric strips has been stitched over this from corner to corner and the resulting diamonds have been filled with spirals of alternating purple and gold, and random shaggy flowers.

A bedroom pillow is judged by what lies beneath its case; the decorative pillow by what covers it.

A dining room needs more than a table and chairs since eating is merely an incidental function of its true purpose . . . a place for your family to share the events from their day, a spot to watch the sun rise in the morning while sipping a cup of coffee, a clear space to help your children with their homework. It's a room that needs personal touches since so many personal needs are met within its walls.

THE DINING ROOM

QUILTED PLACE MAT

QUILTED PLACE MAT

MATERIALS
- Lining fabric
- Cotton print fabric
- Sewing thread: yellow, orange, rust–red
- Assorted remnants of colored polyester
- Fusible webbing
- Cardboard heart templates
- ¼ in (6 mm) batting
- Orange cotton fabric
- Lining fabric for backing

ONCE UPON A TIME, no meal was properly dressed unless there was a whole panoply of tablecloths, mats, napkins, napkin rings, coasters, and 23 varieties of cutlery. Fortunately, those days are gone, and we can now indulge in the luxury of choice – every now and then it is just festive and fun to deck your dinner table with a few additional touches of original linens. These quilted mats will forgive a flattened soufflé and fulfill the practical function of protecting your table finish from hot plates. It makes sense to choose your fabrics with washability in mind so that your mats do not become a culinary journal.

Hearty Meals
A feast of luscious color and exuberant design is guaranteed to bring the often overlooked and undervalued ingredient of finesse to your dining room

A table mat is both a frame and a canvas for your meal. Unlike a painting, however, when you are finished it should be washed before your contributions to its surface can dry.

ASSEMBLING THE GRID

Assembling the fabric

Cut out a rectangle of lining fabric measuring approximately 17 x 13 in (42.5 x 32.5 cm). Tear strips of cotton print fabric in (12 mm) wide and the length or width of the rectangle. Lay them on the rectangle to form a grid pattern consisting of six squares. Pin into position.

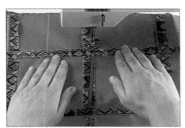

2 **Stitching the grid strips**
Using yellow sewing thread, machine-stitch the grid strips into position with two rows of straight stitching. Remove the pins.

ADDING DECORATION

1 **Cutting out motifs**
Back three small pieces of colored polyester with fusible webbing (see page 12). Using cardboard templates, cut out one large and one small heart from each piece. Peel off the fusible webbing paper backing and iron the hearts onto the grid, alternating the colors in each square.

2 **Stitching motifs**
Cut out a piece of batting the same size as the fabric rectangle; pin the fabric to this. Using a darning foot on the machine and with the presser foot down, stitch the hearts to the fabric rectangle with a straight stitch around the edges, using orange sewing thread.

3 **Quilting the mat**
Stitch narrow strips of orange cotton fabric over the cotton print strips with yellow thread. Quilt each square with tiny yellow or rust-red stitch "knots." Snip off thread ends.

4 **Backing the mat**
Stitch squares of ocher polyester over each grid intersection. Stitch backing fabric to the table mat, right sides together, leaving a gap. Turn right side out; slipstitch the gap closed.

*M*eat and vegetables, pastas and pastries. Some require a few minutes of attention, others much longer. Decorative touches should highlight a kitchen but never hinder your work and its real purpose.

THE
KITCHEN

DECORATED PLANT POTS

DECORATED PLANT POTS

MATERIALS
- Terra-cotta plant pots
- White latex paint
- Acrylic water-based varnish
- Masking tape
- Blue pencil
- Blue acrylic paint
- Acrylic water-based glaze
- Paper motif
- Paper glue

THERE ARE FEW domestic sights more depressing than a kitchen windowsill sporting ugly plastic pots containing moldering mint or blighted basil plants. On the other hand, a crisp battalion of terra-cotta painted to match your kitchen, and spilling over with aromatic herbs, is a great incentive to cook with a bit more panache. And if a green thumb eludes you, painted pots make great containers for kitchen paraphernalia. The combination of paint and découpage is easy and effective. The simple expedient of sealing the base coat with acrylic varnish before you attempt anything requiring dexterity makes the entire procedure far less overwhelming since you can rectify any mistakes.

Pot Checks
If you have a sunny kitchen window, you can grow your own parsley, basil, chervil, and cilantro with which to transform your salads. With no sun, you might grow some handsome potted ivy – which will also help to rid your kitchen of chemical vapors, according to a NASA study.

PAINTING THE POT

1 Outlining tape strips
Paint the pot with two coats of white latex paint. When dry, seal with varnish and allow to dry. Stick evenly spaced strips of masking tape vertically down the pot. Using a blue pencil, mark the edges of the tape on the pot. Peel off the tape, then stick strips of tape horizontally around the pot, and outline with pencil.

2 Painting stripes
Mix some blue acrylic paint with a little acrylic scumble glaze (which slows down the drying time of the paint). Using an artist's brush, paint the vertical stripes down the pot, following the penciled lines. Allow to dry, then paint the horizontal stripes in the same way. If you make a mistake, simply wash it off.

ADDING DECORATION

3 Varnishing the pot
Varnish the decorated pot with three coats of acrylic water-based varnish, allowing each coat to dry before applying the next.

1 Applying a paper cutout
Cut out a paper motif, such as a flower or piece of fruit, from wrapping paper or a magazine. Brush paper glue onto the side of the pot, then stick the motif in position.

2 Sponging off glue
Using a sponge, press the motif into place, easing out any air bubbles and wiping away excess glue. Allow the glue to dry.

*C*onsider decorating your pots with images that reflect their function. A utensil holder, a planter for herbs, or a flower pot can be like tags at the end of garden rows: small billboards that proudly state the obvious.

A study is the best place to reacquaint yourself with some old friends . . . friends like Keats, Dickinson, Twain, and Thoreau. The more intimate your surroundings the more time you'll want to spend in their enlightening company.

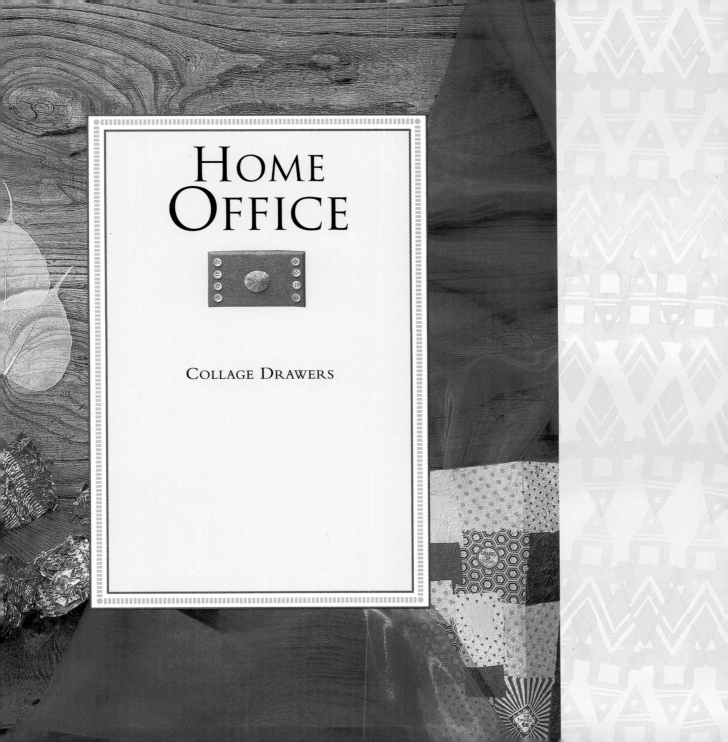

HOME OFFICE

COLLAGE DRAWERS

COLLAGE DRAWERS

MATERIALS
- Set of small wooden drawers
- Used stamps
- Terra-cotta latex paint
- Water
- Wallpaper paste
- Gold paint
- Water-based matte varnish

NO ONE REACHES adulthood without accumulating a wealth of necessary clutter in the form of paper clips, rubber bands, staplers, pens, and pencils – all the paraphernalia that can never be found when you need it, and requires a baffling struggle with the contents of your desk to retrieve. This enchanting little set of drawers is the answer, although you will then have to struggle with other members of your family who recognize it as just the thing in which to keep makeup, jewelry, nuts and bolts, and all the other small, messy essentials of civilized life. You can safely say that you have put your stamp on this one, but you might be prepared – if everyone is very well behaved and duly grateful – to make one or two others as required.

Stamp Collectio[n]

Stamps are not just min[or] works of art, they also co[me] with memories attache[d]. This colorful collage m[ay] well remind you of fo[nd] foreign corresponden[ce] and postcards redole[nt] of fun in the su[n]. If your letters tend to be only flags waving in t[he] breeze, you could relieve [the] unalloyed patriotism [by] using photocopied sectio[ns] of the letters themselv[es].

A decorative drawer is the perfect spot for items you frequently misplace . . .

DECORATING THE DRAWERS

1 Soaking the stamps
Soak the stamps in a bowl of water for 2–3 minutes. Then carefully peel them off their envelope backing. Place the wet stamps down flat to dry, glue side facing upward so that they do not stick to the surface.

2 Painting the drawers
Paint the drawers inside and out with a coat of terra-cotta latex paint. When dry, apply a second coat and let dry.

3 Gluing on the stamps
Rub wallpaper paste onto the back of the stamps with your fingers, and place them on the drawers, abutting them tightly to cover the outside of the drawers; leave the drawer knobs, the inside, and the base of the drawers uncovered. Smooth the stamps down to remove any air bubbles. Wipe off excess glue with a soft cloth. Let dry.

4 Painting drawer knobs
Using an artist's brush, pain[t] the drawer knobs with gold paint and allow to dry. Coa[t] the drawers with water-base[d] matte varnish to seal.

DESIGN OPTIONS

Quick on the Draw

*A parade of sequins and a decorative button
handle would make the perfect drawer front for
a jewelry box. A gardener might like storing
seed packets in drawers decorated with pressed
leaves, and sewing supplies are perfect for storing in drawers edged with tiny mother-of-pearl
buttons and opened with a shell.*

*. . . unless you're never able to
remember where you parked
your car.*

*T*he bedroom – the place where
dreams are born. Give your
imagination a gentle boost before
drifting off to sleep by decorating
with curtains and curios that are as
interesting by moonlight as they are
during the day.

THE
BEDROOM

STAMPED CURTAIN

STAMPED CURTAIN

MATERIALS
- Paper
- Cardboard
- PVA glue
- Block of wood
- Fabric paints
- Plain muslin or cotton curtain

FABRIC PRINTING DOES NOT have to be complicated to be effective. This curtain is simply stamped with a cardboard stamp cut in the shape of a fleur-de-lis, in two colors on plain muslin. The result is clean, stylish, and modern. A crisp repeating design like this, applied with easily available fabric paint that can be fixed with an iron, makes customized furnishings a possibility for everyone. Muslin is a good starting point, because it is cheap and has a pleasant character of its own. You need not fear making the odd mistake with a fabric that costs the same per yard as a cup of coffee. The one drawback is that it does tend to shrink, so you would be wise to prewash it, which unfortunately implies hours of patient ironing.

MAKING AND USING THE STAMP

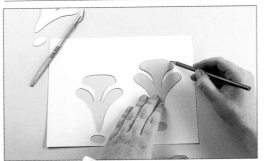

1 Cutting out motifs
Draw a simple fleur-de-lis shape onto a piece of paper. This will be your stamping motif. Cut it out carefully, then draw around the shape twice onto thick cardboard. Cut out the two identical motifs with a craft knife. Repeat this process to make a simple border motif.

2 Making the blocks
Using PVA glue, stick the two identical cardboard shapes together for each motif. Then glue each motif to a separate small block of wood to create stamping blocks.

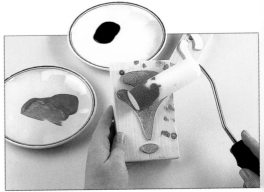

3 Inking up the block
Pour some fabric paint into a saucer. Using a foam paint roller, apply paint to the stamping block; too much paint might cause the print to smudge. Do a few trial prints before stamping the curtain.

Calico Swags

Simple stamps are not difficult to make, and you can use them to print fabric in a spare and elegant style, or use bright colors, irregular placing, and overprinting if you favor something slightly more hectic. In the wake of Walt Disney, you might be able to persuade your dog to run over an ink pad, and then tap-dance on your fabric. Alternatively, you might just make a witty stampable version of animal paw prints with which to print your curtains.

To paraphrase the old adage, be sure to measure the space for your curtains twice before making the first cut in your fabric.

4 Stamping the pattern
Lay the calico curtain on a work surface and press the stamping block evenly on the fabric. Lift up the block carefully to reveal the stamped motif. Repeat to decorate the entire curtain, inking up the block for every print.

5 Stamping the border
Stamp a second motif around the edges of the curtain in a contrasting color, ensuring that you align the stamping block each time. When you have completed the printing, allow the fabric paint to dry, then iron the reverse side of the fabric with a hot iron to fix the paints.

*F*or about an hour each day, most bathrooms have nearly the same climate as a tropical rainforest: hot and steamy. Decorative touches that cannot be thrown into a washing machine or wiped clean with a damp cloth should be kept to a minimum.

THE
BATHROOM

DECORATED GLASS BOTTLES

DECORATED GLASS BOTTLES

MATERIALS
- Glass bottle and stopper
- Turpentine
- Glass paint
- Outline relief paste

RICH, TRANSLUCENT COLORS – bright blue and ruby red, with a filigree of festive gold – make transforming plain glass bottles into Renaissance treasures as easy as painting by numbers. Simple and delicate patterns of dots and stripes, stars and hearts, flowers and leaves are all done in a matter of moments and give clear glass the dazzle of Aladdin's cave. Pretty perfume bottles and jars are often among the inexpensive booty to be found in antique shops. Using the same technique, you can decorate humble drinking glasses and jars to make jewel-like votive lights for your table, or for twilight dining in the garden. Or you can embellish bowls and vases, and tackle glazed door panels with the stained-glass colors of a Gothic cathedral.

PAINTING A BOTTLE

1 Removing grease
To remove grease and fingermarks, wipe the bottle and stopper with a clean, soft cloth dipped in turpentine.

2 Painting the bottle
Apply glass paint with a fine brush, covering the bottle as evenly as possible. Rinse the brush periodically in turpentine. Coat the stopper in a contrasting color. Let dry.

3 Adding outline designs
Decorate the painted surfaces with simple designs drawn in outline relief paste, applied directly from the tube.

Glowing Color
A decorative painted design transforms a simple stoppered perfume bottle into a gem.

Jeweled Treasures

A spectrum of sparkling, clear colors gives glowing life to a collection of bottles of all shapes and characters. The motifs are simple, for often the simplest ideas — like small gold dots on plain midnight blue — are the most effective, and they need no more skill than a steady hand and a confident touch.

With enough imagination it's easy to turn commonplace items into tasteful and inexpensive adornments.

35

*T*he porch and garden are where your personal flair and Nature's rich tapestry meet. Incorporating accents and motifs on your porch or patio that reflect the colors and patterns of your garden or lawn will add just the right finishing touches to your carefully designed home.

THE
PORCH
& GARDEN

MOSAIC TABLETOP

MOSAIC TABLETOP

MATERIALS
- Circular wooden tabletop and metal base
- Ceramic tiles
- PVA glue
- Strip of lead, the circumference of the tabletop
- Nails
- Gray tile grout
- Marker

Mosaic scissors

THIS SPARKLING TABLETOP is a real *pièce de résistance*. Tackle it fearlessly and with gusto; mosaic is not difficult, it just needs patience, a bold design for success, and a pair of goggles for safety. For the thrifty-minded, it is a wonderfully economic way to use up the odd, chipped, and broken tiles that stores are eager to sell off. Make sure that the tiles are all the same thickness and finish, though, or the surface of the table will be uneven. Here the central motif is made up of larger, distinct triangles to give emphasis and crisp definition. A small object like this tabletop can look somewhat chaotic unless the color range is limited. The tiles here are confined to complementary nautical blues and white. The fillet of lead around the tabletop makes a neat, easy, and professional-looking finish.

Mariner's Mosaic
A seafarer's compass inspire *this table, a strong motif in* *variety of cool blues that* *would be the perfect perch* *for a croissant and coffee in* *the garden, or a plant or tw* *in the porch.*

A mosaic tabletop is a wonderful project for the whole family to enjoy. Once you have established a pattern, the mosaic is like a jigsaw puzzle with each person contributing pieces that soon become a colorful image.

PREPARING THE MOSAIC

1 Drawing design outline
Using a marker , draw a simple design for the mosaic on top of the circular tabletop. This compass design is composed of triangles and concentric circles.

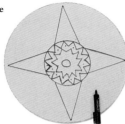

2 Cutting tiles
Using mosaic scissors, cut ceramic tiles into small pieces for the central design, and rectangles for the border circles. Wear goggles to protect your eyes while cutting the tiles.

APPLYING THE MOSAIC AND EDGING

1 Building up the pattern
Use a spatula to apply PVA glue onto the marked central design on the tabletop. Place pieces of tile onto the glue, leaving a slight gap between pieces, to build up the central pattern (see inset). Then build up the surrounding area with a pattern of circles. Use the mosaic scissors to "nibble" the tiles into smaller shapes as desired.

2 Edging with lead
Wrap a strip of lead around the tabletop and cut it to fit exactly, using a pair of scissors. Secure the lead to the tabletop by hammering in nails at 4in (10cm) intervals around the circumference, and then a couple at each end.

3 Grouting the mosaic
Leave the mosaic to dry for a day. Apply gray tile grout (mixed to mud pie consistency) over the mosaic with a squeegee. Clean off the excess with a damp cloth or sponge. When dry, polish with a soft cloth and attach the tabletop to the base.

DESIGN OPTIONS

Concentric Circles
Circles of speckled color in sea greens and stone combine in a very simple but effective design.

Scarlet Starburst
An entire rainbow of color making a graduated star is here enclosed in a rim of bright yellow.

C.R.Gibson®
FINE GIFTS SINCE 1870

This book is based on *Complete Home Crafts*,
first published in Great Britain in 1997
by Dorling Kindersley Limited, London

Developed by Matthew A. Price, Nashville, Tennessee.

Published by C. R. Gibson®
C. R. Gibson® is a registered trademark of Thomas Nelson, Inc.
Norwalk, Connecticut 06856

Printed in Singapore by Star Standard.

ISBN 0–7667–6163–0
UPC 082272–44984–8
GB4140

PICTURE CREDITS
Photography by Clive Streeter.

ACKNOWLEDGMENTS
The following companies kindly loaned antiques and bric-à-brac for photography:
Magpies, 152 Wandsworth Bridge Road, Fulham, London SW6 2UH. Tel: 0171-736 3738